The Halloween Business

Double Your Income,
Work 2 Months Per Year,
Without Quitting Your Job

Shannon Shue

ISBN-13: 978-0615891972
ISBN-10: 0615891977
Copyright © 2013 by Shannon Shue

The Halloween Business

Double Your Income,
Work 2 Months Per Year,
Without Quitting Your Job

Shannon Shue

Acknowledgements

Many people contributed to the making of this book. It is a huge undertaking to write a book. This book is possible because of the love and support of:

My mom, Beverly Shue, who gave me roots and wings

Clint Author, who kicked my ass and believes whole-heartedly in me

Sonya Lott-Harrison, who shared a big part of this journey with me

Shaun, my brother, who is a constant force of calm and good

Sara Kurtzenhauser, who writes me hand written letters of encouragement

My partner, Mira "MJ" Johnson, who is the wind in my sails and my greatest inspiration

And to you, the entrepreneur,

"Go confidently in the direction of your dreams! Live the life you imagined!" - Thoreau

Preface

I never thought I would write a book-especially about succeeding in the Halloween Business. I did not see myself as a great writer. But I knew I had valuable information that if shared could change the lives of more people than I had previously dreamed. So, despite my fear of writing, I have written this book.

My long-time friend from college Resa and her husband were a part of this inspiration for this book. Resa's husband had lost his architecture job after the 2008 economic crash and they were surviving on one income. They had lost a lot of equity in their home and an investment property. They were also trying to cope with ballooning mortgage loans on both homes. They managed to keep their home, but sold the investment property at a loss.

To make things more challenging, Resa's son Kirk was diagnosed with a learning disability. They wanted to provide him with specialized early education that would prepare him for pre-school and the rest of his life. Before Resa's husband lost his job and the 2008 real estate crash, specialized education wouldn't have been a financial burden.

While they had never been entrepreneurs, they wanted to start a business. They asked if I would give them advice on starting a Halloween online store. It became a personal mission for me to mentor them and help them to get back on their feet financially. More than anything, I wanted to be sure Kirk got the special education he needed as early as possible.

I am happy to report they are now doing great financially. Kirk is doing fantastic in school. He loves math and excels in geography. The success of this business here in the United States inspired them to look at continuing their success abroad. Resa's husband is a native of Peru. They are planning to start a year round store in Lima. In Peru, the economy is booming and they will be able to continue providing Kirk with a top-notch special education at international schools.

It feels so rewarding to be a part of their success and to create this book from our journey. In addition to success stories like this one, this book was built on my many years of experiences as a sales and marketing executive in the Halloween industry. I learned about every aspect of the Halloween industry; investment planning, costume design, online marketing, merchandising, and overseas production. I offer the information in this book, TheHalloweenBusiness.com consulting programs and one-on-one success masterminds to you so that you will be able to build a Halloween business and have the confidence needed to thrive. This is our start to something great together!

TIP BOX: Throughout the book, I will use these boxes to indicate key information or online videos to help you get started. Check out my welcome video:
www.thehalloweenbusiness.com/book/welcome

TABLE OF CONTENTS

PART 1
OVERVIEW OF
THE HALLOWEEN
BUSINESSS

CHAPTER 1: THE ENTREPRENEURIAL OPPORTUNITY

Why start a Halloween business? There is a simple answer- to have fun and make money in a short period of time.

I love it when people ask, "What do you do?" I reply 'I work in the Halloween Business.' There are two distinct reactions. One reaction is "Wow, I love Halloween. This year I want to dress up as a steam punk coolie and last year I went as Angelina Jolie Octo-mom." The other distinct reaction is "Wow, what do you do the rest of the year, when it isn't Halloween?"

Both of these reactions are amazing. They convey exactly what everyone feels about dressing up. They think it is creative and tons of fun or they think I hardly work. People love dressing up because you get to be someone else. People also love to work less and enjoy life more.

POPULARITY OF HALLOWEEN

The entire Halloween industry is built on fun. Dressing up as a character allows individuals to use their creativity and be outside of themselves for a day. The fantasy and fun associated with dressing up and socializing creates great memories.

In the United States, Halloween is a very lucrative holiday, second only to Christmas. It is the time of the year where there is the most amount of money to be made in the shortest period of time. In October many stores experience a rush to get a costume at the last minute, just like last minute Christmas shoppers.

However Halloween did not come from the United States. It originated from the Christians in Western Europe. It is also referred to as *All Hallow's Eve*. Traditionally a feast was served on this holiday. The customs of carving root vegetables (originally turnips) and wearing costumes were European traditions. Halloween and variations on the tradition, such as carving a pumpkin instead of a turnip) began in the United States in the 19th century when a large number of people from Ireland and Scotland came to the United States. By the beginning of the 20th century Halloween had become a mainstream holiday throughout the United States.

Today, Halloween is an international phenomenon. This international development of Halloween in new markets has enabled entrepreneurs from around the world to make money and introduce other cultures to a fun holiday. So now, celebrating Halloween anywhere is an opportunity to get together with friends and have fun. For adults, it is also a reminder of their younger years when as children they went "trick or treating." For parents, Halloween is an occasion to help their children dress up and create fun memories.

The fun associated with dressing up and stepping outside of oneself for a day has also extended beyond its origin of Halloween. The whole world is having more parties, for the work place, special events and themes around holidays. As a result, the sales of costumes and décor for these other occasions allow many businesses to make money year-round.

TYPES OF HALLOWEEN STORES

There are three types of stores in which you can sell Halloween products; online, temporary, and year-round. An **online store** is the least expensive start-up as you only need internet access and space in your residence. You can sell on an established marketplace like Amazon or eBay, or you can create your own website. The Halloween market is growing outside of the United States. So having an online store will give you access to a larger buying audience. A **temporary store** is a brick and mortar store that is open from mid-September until a few days after Halloween. This business model is very successful in the United States because most costumes and décor for Halloween are sold in a single month. A **year-round store** is also called a *party store* because party items for many different themes are sold throughout the year.

PROFITS

The tools provided in this book and on TheHalloweenBusiness.com websites are designed to make it easy for you to double the money you invest in

Halloween costumes and decorations in as little as two months. There is no stock or other business opportunity that will give you this type of return. I have worked with clients who started with a few thousand dollars and increased their profits to a million dollars in two years. However, this is a not a get rich quick scheme or a one-time business deal in which you invest a lot of money for a few months and then you never have to work again.

I am presenting a business opportunity that you will operate for a few months each year that will generate a second income while you maintain a day job or one that you will run as a full time business and eventually train other people to take care of the day to day business responsibilities. But you will have to get the business started and do the hard work to be successful.

COMPETITION

Competition is inevitable in business. Accept competition at the beginning of your business endeavor and learn how to gain a competitive advantage. There are three ways to increase your competitive advantage in business; price, customer service; and unique product position. If you have two out of the three of these working for you, your competitors will stand up and take notice of your Halloween business. If you only have one of these three factors in place, then you will not be successful. Focusing solely on price as a way to beat out your competition is like a race to the bottom. Offering the lowest price won't sustain a business because as soon as you are not the cheapest, you lose business. Customers who shop for the lowest price are not brand loyal. You can create brand loyalty by building a unique product offering. Each of these components of a successful business will be discussed in later chapters of this book.

Competition varies depending on the country in which you are starting your Halloween business. While brick and mortar and online stores are well established in the US and Canada, there is still room for new competition and growth in these established markets. In Europe, Asia, South America and Oceania the competition is just beginning. I have worked with hundreds of entrepreneurs from around the world that are having success in the Halloween business.

CHAPTER 2: SUCCESS

DEFINING YOUR SUCCESS

A new business is risky and you will be putting your time and energy into a new endeavor. All of the entrepreneurs I have worked with are smart, driven and calculated risk takers. You are just like them. You want to be successful too.

When you start a new business, it is important to define what success means to you and establish some clear goals. These goals are the key ingredients for creating the outcomes you want. These clearly articulated outcomes will be the tangible way whereby you will measure success. So, I would like you to think about the questions below. It would be useful to write down your responses.

1. Why do I want to go into business for myself?
2. What do I want to accomplish in selling Halloween?
3. What areas of my life do I need to work on?
4. How much money do I want to make in my first year?
5. What would I like to learn in starting my own business?

SKILLS NEEDED FOR SUCCESS

Starting a business takes a village of talent. In the beginning, most business owners wear many hats; accountant, customer service representative, and janitor. The most successful entrepreneur is open to acquiring the skills needed to run a business. One of the first skills I want you to learn is to make it easier on yourself by asking for help when you needed it. For example, if you are not comfortable making fashion decisions about costumes, you should consult with friends or family who may know more about costume trends. I offer one-on-one, group and home study programs on skill building and excelleration to achieving your dream business at TheHalloweenbusiness.com. Programs start as little as $80/month and short as 6-weeks for those dedicated to greatness.

Another important skill is learning to delegate work to others, especially when they are more knowledgeable about or skilled in a particular job. Finally, teach your staff the skills you have mastered. If you are an excellent sales person, you should train others to be excellent sales people.

The required skills are defined in this chapter. Some skills are only required for one type of store, whereas others are needed in all three types of stores. Do not feel obligated to master each skill before starting the business. You will learn as you go. You already possess some of the skills. You will learn the others as you get started in your business.

BUYING

Buying can be especially challenging for some Halloween business owners. In order to become a top notch buyer of costumes and accessories you will need to follow pop culture fashion trends. You will need to learn about the fabrics, colors, patterns, and cuts that are in style at any given time. Don't worry if you are "fashion challenged," you will be able to learn a lot about fashion in a short amount of time.

SALES

Persuading individuals to buy your product is the most important skill to learn. Selling product to people, even if it is not what they wanted or something they had not given thought to buying is a greater skill. This skill is referred to as up-selling. An example of this would be persuading a customer who came to your online or brick and mortar store only to buy fake blood to also purchase a pair of red contact lenses and a zombie make up kit. In this example, you would have made a sale that was three times the amount the customer originally intended to spend. Now that is a talent!

MERCHANDISING

Merchandising involves creating a shopping experience that will convert a potential customer into a paying customer based on how products are visually displayed and how easy it is to find costumes and accessories. Store merchandising will increase sales and assist in selling additional accessories with costumes. In a physical store, effective merchandising includes setting up store window displays and organizing the store shelves to maximize the number of costumes being displayed. For an online store, merchandising involves making your website visually appealing and easy to navigate. You want customers to be able to find what they want without much help.

INVENTORY MANAGEMENT

It is important to keep track of the product that is purchased and delivered from suppliers, how quickly it sells, and what is not really selling. I strongly recommend using a point-of-sale inventory management program.

Point-of-sale (POS) computer software programs give you information about live inventory of sales and stock. This is how you manage your daily, weekly and monthly inventory. This information enables you to compare sales, like the weekend versus the weekday, the evening versus the afternoon or the first week of October versus the last week of October. The POS will let you know when you need to reorder popular product that is selling quickly. It will also let you know what is selling slowly. This knowledge will inform you when it is time to lower the prices to move inventory faster. Another advantage of using a point-of-sale computer program is that it can control theft. All of this information will help you be more successful each year you do business. I suggest considering these retail POS software programs that can handle multiple items using touch screen technology for registers and integrates with most accounting software, AccuPOS, Shopkeeper and POSGuys. Think of a POS software programs as your business life line.

CLOTHING MANUFACTURING

Some knowledge of how clothing is manufactured-the craftsmanship, the materials used and the durability will help you to avoid buying cheaper quality costumes than what manufacturers may advertise. In the Halloween industry, many products are made inexpensively in Asia, so quality varies greatly. Sometimes the product samples at big industry shows are made with higher quality materials than the mass produced costumes that are shipped.

ACCOUNTING

This is probably the least favorite of all the tasks for any business owner, unless you are an accountant. But it is so important to account for all sales and costs of running the business. You need to be aware of your profits and losses so you can remain profitable working within your budget. You also need to be knowledgeable about your tax obligations. I strongly recommend working with an accountant for all of these tasks.

MARKETING

This skill is one of the key areas in order to build a following, for customers to find you online or in stores. Common marketing methods are social media, websites, printed fliers, advertising in local newspapers, Search Engine Optimization (SEO) by key words, sign twirlers outside the store, television or radio ads, writing copy for products online and word of mouth. Marketing in each of these categories is either a cost of time or money. I recommend you start with two or three areas to promote your business. For online stores, a website, good copy for product descriptions and SEO are the most important to succeed. For a physical store location, a website, local publicity, social media and fliers are important. As you build your business, you will begin to master the most important marketing areas, and then be able to take on media and publicity for additional marketing.

EMPLOYEE MANAGEMENT

When you have a store or a warehouse, hiring honest, organized and hard-working people is essential. Generally, this is not a problem when you hire your family and friends. As your business grows or if your family and friends are not reliable, you will need to hire other employees. You will need to learn how to recognize good candidates for the positions that will need to be filled. You will also need good leadership skills to oversee and motivate your employees.

SECURITY

For brick and mortar stores security is a very important part of your business. Cash registers often have cameras to discourage employees from stealing. But depending on the size of your store staff, you may want to have more of a security presence to prevent employee and customer theft as well as crowd control in the days leading up to Halloween.

REAL ESTATE

You should work with a commercial retail agent if you are planning to open a temporary store, year-round store or warehouse space. However, do not rely solely on the agent, you should learn as much as you can about real estate. This will allow you to find and work with the best agents for your business. Knowledge about real estate is also useful if you need to engage in bidding with competing temporary chain stores for the same prime locations.

MEASURING SUCCESSFUL SALES

I measure quantitative success by sell-through percentages using the old school grading system. Sell through is the amount of product you sell. For example, if you have $1000 in product to sell and you sell $900, you have a 90% sell through. The remaining $100 dollars was not sold and is left over inventory. See Table 2.1 for the Sell Through Grading System.

Table 2.1 Sell Through Grading System

SELLING GRADE	EXPLANATION	RECOMMENDATION
A = 90% +	Excellent! Could have made more money with more product	Repeat this momentum next year.
B = 80-89%	Great job! This is the level you aim to reach each year.	Repeat this momentum next year.

C = 70-79%	This is average.	You have created a successful business but continue selling and aim for 80%
D = 60-69% F= 60% or below	This is below average. There is a good chance you lost money and have too much left over product. You may not have been able to cover your overhead or pay your suppliers or both.	If this is your first year in business, then do not despair, and work to sell through to 70-80% next year. If it is your 2nd or 3rd year in the business, this is a concern but it's possible that if you sell your current inventory next year and not buy too many new products you can make a profit.

If this is your second or third year in business and you are still operating at a D level or F level selling, then I recommend you work with me to help you sell more of your inventory and meet all of your financial obligations.

Once all of your bills are paid and you are generating a healthy profit it will be time to turn your attention to a qualitative measure of success. Eventually, you want to get the business to be a passive income generator with a knowledgeable general manager in place to handle the day-to-day operations. That leaves you to act on big problems like building maintenance, employee disagreements and sales performance. This means you do not have to work as hard and will be freed up to focus on other entrepreneurial endeavors and spend more time having fun.

CHAPTER 3: YEAR-ROUND PLANNING

Each year Halloween costume and décor companies design new products. As in the fashion world, they reveal these costumes at large Halloween industry shows throughout the United States and Europe. Most of the industry shows happen between January and March. These companies want to secure your order early enough to plan production. Orders received by March give the overseas manufacturers time to make new product for Halloween. If your supplier receives your order early, they can account for what you will need in August and September for Halloween. So even if you have a temporary store, you will still need to engage in year-round planning activities. I encourage you to strive for this schedule so you work with your suppliers to maximize product delivery and customer service. Table 1 outlines the year round activities of manufacturers and scheduled activities for store owners.

PLANNING THE WORK

Table 1-Year Round Planning Schedule for Vendors, Suppliers, and Buyers

	Vendors & Suppliers	Buyers
January-February	Creating early projections for annual product quantities. Encouraging buyers to order early so you spend more of your budget with them.	Visiting shows to see the new costume lines and ordering early to receive discounts.
March-April	Sending purchase orders to their factories and finalizing the designs of the new line.	Planning store location or beginning to upload items purchased onto your website.
May-June	Getting product in the warehouse to prepare for Halloween and shipping to customers.	Receiving early shipments of product. If you have a temporary store, you are negotiating for store space or signing a lease. For online stores, putting up all the new images and descriptions in preparation for Halloween.

July-August	Shipping large amounts of product to you in multiple orders, with some items already on backorder.	Receiving orders from early online shopping. For brick and mortar stores, hiring and training staff for setting up the store. Receiving large shipments, putting them into your point-of-sale system and organizing the set-up of items into your inventory.
September-October	Shipping last minute re-orders and backorders. They are creating and finalizing the new line of costumes, accessories and décor for the next year.	Setting up your store and experiencing a rapid increase in sales. You will also begin re-ordering top selling costumes and accessories.

This simple organization of work flow between you and your vendors will help you understand the bigger picture. Placing your orders early for Halloween will result in greater success. I have worked with many new Halloween business owners who wait until August or September to start ordering merchandise and planning their store. This adds a level of uncertainty with your orders being fulfilled by vendors and the manufacturers to have product shipped in time for Halloween. Manufacturers want to sell more products, so they prefer early orders. They always include additional quantities for late orders, but it is difficult to predict popular items accurately and how many late orders are received. When you order late, you are being given what is available. But if you are reading this book weeks or months before Halloween, it is really never too late to order from suppliers. Buy the top selling available items to get started and use the tools in this book to know what to expect and how to handle challenges that arise.

MAPPING SALES TRENDS

The two months of the year during which you will work the hardest- September and October- are also the months in which you will make the most money. Table 2 illustrates the breakdown of sales activities in the last five weeks before Halloween. When viewing Table 2 you will notice that the greatest number of sales and profits are happening in the fourth week of Halloween for stores and third week of Halloween for online retailers.

Table 2-Mapping Sales Trends

Week	Temporary and Year Round Stores	Online
September 26-October 3	5%	5%
October 4-10	10%	10%
October 11-16	20%	25%
October 17-23	25%	40%
October 24-30	40%	20%

For brick and mortar stores, the highest number of sales happens in the fourth week of October. These are sales from the same type of customers that do all of their Christmas shopping on Christmas Eve. Your work hours will triple in the fourth week compared to the first week of October to accommodate late shoppers. Expect to have extra staff and extended hours during the last few weeks before Halloween. It will be exciting and overwhelming at the same time and this will keep you and your staff coming back season after season.

For online sales, the momentum picks up in the third week of October and begins to wane in the fourth week. This is because shoppers need to order far enough in advance to receive their costume by Halloween without having to pay for express shipping.

TIP BOX: For shipping calculate, the longest distance between two major cities in your country to decide the number of days to ship. During the last week before Halloween, it is really important to get orders delivered reliably and on time. If their orders arrive after Halloween, these customers will be more inclined to post bad reviews about your business on the Internet and never buy from you again.

POST HALLOWEEN PLANNING

The day after Halloween you will be exhausted. You will wake up facing an entire store clean-up and inventory. If you are in a temporary store, you will need to pack up all the costumes. For a Year-Round store, you will need to pack away the scary, bloody and horror costumes for next year. Taking inventory will allow you to know what sold well and inform your buying decisions for next year. As you get better at planning, the process of buying gets easier. Even if you do did not have time to plan far enough in advance for a successful first Halloween season, you will be more successful next Halloween season as a result of this experience. Planning during the low season requires fewer hours and so it resembles more of a part time job. Independent of the type of store you open, each year you will grow as an entrepreneur and plan better for the next year. It is important to measure your success by having clear goals. Learning more about the business should be one of those goals. This business gives you time to reflect. Use it.

PART 2
TAKE ACTION

CHAPTER 3: GETTING STARTED

The startup costs as well as the skills needed to successfully operate a Halloween business will vary depending on the type of store that you choose.

ONLINE STORE

An online store is the least expensive type of Halloween business to start. You only need a computer, a high speed Internet connection and a work space in your home. I recommend beginning with an online store based on the low startup costs. Also online buying and shopping is popular worldwide. In order to have enough time to buy the products you need and set your store up online, you should start your online store at least 4 months before Halloween.

There are two places to start an online store, your own website or an established online retailer. Creating your own website is more initial work. However you have control over search ability and designing an online shopping experience. Using an established online retailer, like Amazon, eBay or Buy.com, allows you to put up your product quickly without have to design a website. This method of selling is price competitive because other retailers are listing the same costumes in the shared online marketplace. It is easy to sort by price and often shoppers look for the lowest cost first. Decide which type of online store you would like to start and you may choose to start both, if you have enough time and money before Halloween to efficiently build the store online.

Amazon and eBay are the most popular marketplaces to sell product and I recommend setting up an account to start selling online. Other companies with an online marketplace are Buy, Newegg, Overstock and Sears have online marketplaces that offer fewer costumes during Halloween, so you can consider other sites. However, I highly recommend an Amazon and eBay account to sell. To set up an Amazon account, simply follow the steps at Amazon.com under by searching for "Sell On Amazon." Their tutorial will walk you through the steps between a professional seller or an individual seller. You should choose professional seller because you will be selling over 40 items a month. As for getting your account set up for eBay.com, go to the "Sell" tab on the homepage to register and start selling product right away. For all online marketplaces, you will be charged an average of 10%-15% for each item sold by the marketplace. This how Amazon or eBay make money. They optimize the searches online to bring sellers to the website to buy your products. This is a cost of doing business and it is standard for online sites. To avoid the fees, you can also create your own website, but you will have to drive buyers to your site through searches.

To create your own branded website you will first need to choose a logo, design, a place to host your site and a domain name. Your logo and first website design should be done professionally. If you are experienced in graphic design and web design, then you should design something spectacular. If not, you can easily hire a designer from ODesk.com or have a design contest on 99designs.com to have you brand started. These are two sites I have used and there are many other similar sites that allow you to find freelance designers. A logo and a website design, should take two to four weeks to complete a basic website start.

TIP BOX: For help creating a website using freelance designers and developers, I recommend check out my website www.thehalloweenbusiness.com/book/freelance for additional resources on hiring talent.

I recommend having your web designer use WordPress.org for the design template. I use WordPress.org exclusively because the websites are easy to start and most web developers are familiar with how to program or customize templates for your needs. WordPress.org templates are highly customizable and give you the potential to expand your website as your sales grow. It is important to note that WordPress.com is not the same website as Word Press.org. WordPress.com is a website host that also offers customizable design templates that are easier to customize because the templates have fewer options. WordPress.com is more limited because it is focused on blogging. Aside from WordPress.com and WordPress.org, there are other platforms for an e-commerce site, so search for the easiest fit for your needs.

For website hosting services that are not included with the purchase of your website, I recently selected HostGator.com for my websites. Once you choose a host, it's a good idea to stay with that host. I tend to call my hosting site a lot when I am first getting set up. So, it's important to choose a hosting site with good customer service and easy access to a real person when there is a problem. The cheaper the hosting the less personalized services you receive.

A domain name is a unique name that you assign to your website. It is the way that Internet users are able to find your website directly. Choose a domain that is easy to remember and fun. Ideally, your domain will be your company name. If your company name isn't available as a domain, try to get a domain that is as close to your company name as possible. For example, if *costumeparty.com* isn't available then try purchasing *funcostumeparty.com*. Always buy a domain name with the .com extension. If you are starting your business outside of the United States, buy the .co or commercial website extension used in your country. I do not recommend buying a domain name with extensions such as .biz, .org, .net or .tv because they are not easy to remember. To make it easier, buy your domain name from your website hosting service. For a quick solution without having to plan out the web development or hosting, buy the site you want on godaddy.com to secure the domain you want.

The next step in setting up your online store is to write the content for each section of your website. Your website should have a home page, a search box, shopping cart, an about page and a contact page. The *about* page is very important. This is your only interaction with potential customers. It is the place to tell customers who you are and why they should buy from you. Be genuine and do not sound like a sales person. Additional pages, such as a blog, social media links and videos can be added later. Another priority is to develop content that will help drive sells. So write a detailed and interesting description of all of the costume categories as well as for each individual costume.

For your first website, place all costumes and decor for Halloween on this site. The products page should be organized into categories by size, gender and genre. Work with your web developer to be able to sort by these categories and also to create a search function from key words you will enter on each costume. A list of suggested genres to use as keywords is provided in chapter 5, Table 5.2. This organization of costumes by individual key words and genre needs to make shopping easy to navigate on your site.

To refine the product pages of your website, each costume should have well organized information. Have a clear layout for the costume or accessory product name, sizes available, description of what is included, a description of the costume's design features and photos of the costume. If you have videos of the item, be sure to include them. Images and videos sell everything, since a customer cannot try the costume on. Have the zoom feature, so shoppers can see details.

Include the side shot and the back shot if you can. The more a shopper sees of the product, the more informed decision they will be able to make on what they will buy.

In the area below the costume, offer other options to consider purchasing to complete the look. This space is called "You May Also Like" (YMALs). The layout helps close the sale by making it easy to add and size the right costume. You should have a link to the size chart with clear measurements for the body on each product page. Some customers will estimate their size based on what they always wear in general and some will study the sizing chart to figure out their size. They will call customer service if they do not know what size to choose so find the right size to minimize returns and confusion with the sizing chart online.

Once you have set up your website and purchased the product from vendors is delivered, you are officially in business. Test your shopping cart, purchase page and shipping process before you go live to the public. It is important to test the site for errors or problems, so you can have minimal issues after your grand opening.

TIP BOX: A newer trend with online stores is to create micro-site stores. These are smaller specific shopping sites. For example, Dinosaur costumes for kids or 1990's costumes. Often these smaller sites are built on the same database as a larger megastore site, but as a way to have multiple sites searchable online.

TEMPORARY STORE

A temporary store may work best for entrepreneurs that have not had retail experience and want a short selling season. A temporary store would be ideal for an entrepreneur with another seasonal business or the flexibility to leave a day job for six weeks and enjoys working in a high pressured, fast paced environment, directly with customers and staff. Typically, it will take a minimum of five months before Halloween to start a temporary store.

The neighborhood and location are crucial to a successful launch of your temporary store. Temporary stores are usually in shopping malls, strip malls or boutique shops. The best place to start a temporary store is in a high traffic and easy to find shopping location in a middle to upper class area. An ideal location is viewable from the street and with easy parking for customers.

Your temporary store will be open for five to eight weeks before Halloween. In a matter of a week, you will "pop-up" a store with shelves, aisles, dressing rooms and registers. Within a few days after Halloween, you will pack up all of your merchandise and move out.

The first task in opening a Halloween store is to find a lease for two months. In the United States this is not an issue. There are an abundance of commercial real estate resources online and locally. When a commercial property has been vacant for a while, owners are eager to rent. In some countries, a two month lease is difficult. Usually, the challenge is rental property taxes, minimum lease agreements or labor laws preventing staff employment for two months. If you are opening a temporary store in a country outside of the United States, you should first check the regulations on temporary store space. Independent of your location, if you can negotiate a two month lease, property owners will more wary of a short term lease, so you should be an ideal tenant. Be clean, be a good neighbor to the other stores and bring shoppers into the mall. This will build trust over time.

TIP BOX: Since a lease agreement is a legal binding contract, it is recommended that you consult with an attorney to review the terms of agreement before signing.

To negotiate for a lease, here are a few areas you can offer to sweeten the deal. Offer fair market price to rent a space, do not low ball an offer. If you really want the space, you can offer to give a percentage of the revenue or profit. Typically, you offer less in rent and 2-4% of profits. This gives the property owner an incentive for success. For example, if a 4,000 square foot retail space usually rents for $7,000 for a long term 3 year lease, offer $8,000. Another option would be to give the building owners a percentage of your gross profits with a lower monthly rental agreement. You could offer $7,000/month for a two month lease, plus an additional 2-3% on the profits if you exceed a certain amount of sales. If you sell $50,000-75,000 in gross profits for a 4,000 square foot space, it is an extra $1000-1800 rent. Some US temporary stores are mega size, at 10,000-20,000 square feet and can profit between $120,000-240,000, in two months.

Figure 3.1: 3 Sample Store Layouts

A 20 foot by 20 foot space (400 square feet). Ideal for small boutiques or inside of a larger retail store with a costume section.

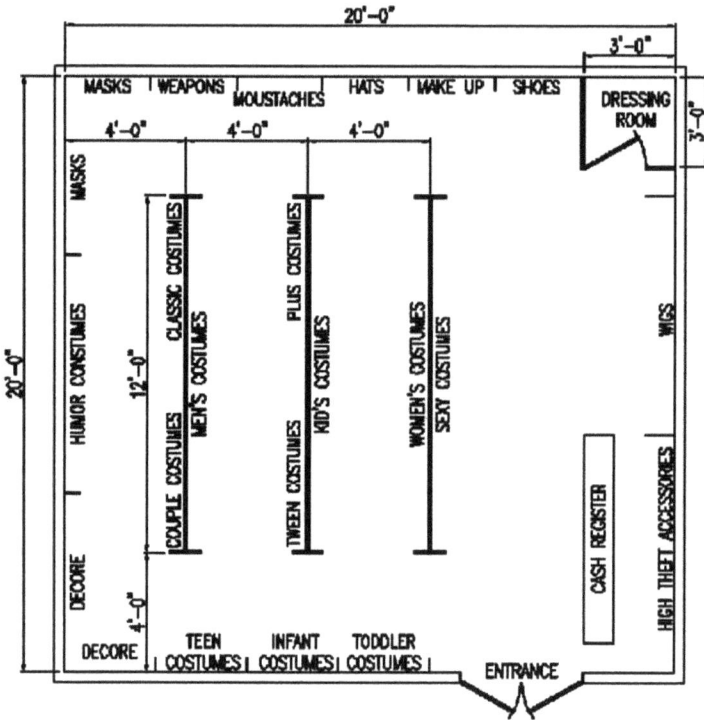

A 40 foot by 40 foot space (1600 square feet). Ideal for a mall or shopping center size retail store dedicated to costumes and décor.

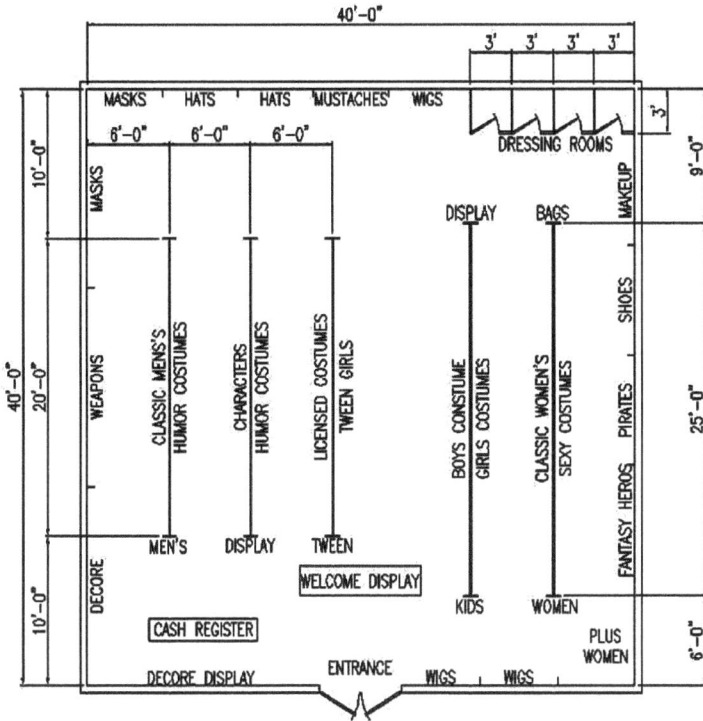

A 90 foot by 56 foot space, (5040 square feet). Ideal for a mega store or a large stand-alone store space in a shopping plaza or strip mall.

With a location secured, it is time to layout your store space. The store layout will be laid out in a manner that leads customers through the store in a general traffic pattern. Costumes should be organized and displayed according to age, size, and type of costume or accessories.

Merchandising for a temporary store requires building the easiest and quickest system using grid wall to make displays. Metal grid wall is usually 2 feet by 6 feet or 8 feet high long. When it is put together with zip ties, it forms a strong wall to hold up hooks and shelves. This is the least expensive material to build aisles. All other options are much heavier and expensive. If you rent a space with shelves or hooks already installed, you have saved yourself some time and money. More information about how to display your products is discussed in the chapter on merchandising.

Buy gridwall from a local supplier or online by searching under the term "buy gridwall" in Google. Expect to pay between $15 and $20 for each gridwall piece of 2x6 or 2x8. Also, buy hooks that attaché to the gridwall to display product. You will need at least ten hooks per gridwall piece. There are various lengths for the hooks, so buy a few of each size and set up a few piece of grid wall with hooks, before your final purchase. Gridwall comes in black, chrome and white colors. To give the gridwall a nicer retail feel, clip fabric to it and the hooks will hang through the gridwall.

YEAR-ROUND STORE

The Halloween business originated as year round stores, originally selling party goods, joke shops and toy shops. Party stores and toy stores made great money for Halloween when a few companies started selling masks and costumes in the late 1970s and early1980s. Many year round stores have been in business for at least 15 years in the United States. A year round store is suited for an entrepreneur who is interested in a long term business investment. A good plan for a year round store is to plan how to market costumes in the off season. Many successful stores sell costumes year round based on holidays and events. Additionally, they offer other party products like balloon sculptures, party rental equipment or party planning services.

A year round store takes a minimum of nine months to set up because you will need to determine the amount of square footage you will need, choose a location, and create a business plan to generate year round revenue. As with the temporary store, the location of the year round store needs to be in a high traffic area, with higher-income family oriented shoppers and easy parking options. The size of the store will vary on how much money you have to spend on a lease and interior design. As it is possible that you will not realize a profit in the first six month, I recommend having six to twelve months of rent and start-up costs after opening the business. This recommendation may seem aggressive, especially since many stores start with much less reserve. However, it takes a few months of marketing to generate a solid paying customer base.

Even though you will be selling other party products, the set up the store for Halloween sales can be similar to setting up a temporary store except that Halloween costumes should be over 70% of your total store product. With a year-round store you have the option of setting up your merchandise to create a more boutique like shopping experience. In fact, the most successful year round stores create a shopping experience and market themselves as unique. This angle will always work regardless of the competition and prices.

The interior design of the store should be theme based to create a particular mood or experience. For example, product can be hung on hangers like a clothing store instead of folded in the plastic bag from the manufacturer. The staff in a year round store will also be more knowledgeable about the product and should be trained to be consultants on accessorizing a costume. As a permanent store, you can have events and market your store to draw celebrity shoppers. Hold events to help promote the business visibility to the local community and have free publicity.

Starting a year round store is more work and usually takes longer to see a return on your investment, but it is truly a worthwhile commitment.

CHAPTER 4: BUY PRODUCT LIKE A PRO

Knowing what to buy, how much to buy and where to buy is a big part of learning to sell costumes and accessories. The Halloween industry is large and consists of costumes, wigs, masks, plastic weapons, fake blood, decorations, haunted house props and make up. Choosing the right combination of products is important for success. But in your first year, in order to simplify the shipments and the number of styles, limit the amount of product you buy and the number of wholesale vendors you buy from. As you grow your business, continue to add more selections, new vendors and manufacturers.

As a new buyer, I recommend you ask for advice from trusted people about costume trends, your sales person from each vendor for the top selling costumes and refer to my website, http://thehalloweenbusiness.com/book/trends for up-to-date trends. My easiest tip for understanding trends is to follow popular TV, music stars and movies to buying trendiest costumes each year. Another area for costume trends by style, color and fashion design are department stores and designer labels. Keep in mind, the Halloween industry trends lag two to three years behind the fashion trends, so if you do not get on board right away, you always have next year to buy the latest trends.

BUYING COSTUMES

For all types of Halloween stores, costumes will be the mainstay of your business. Before you begin buying costumes, you will need to decide if you will offer costumes for all ages, both male, female and accessories or for a smaller segment of the population, like for women only or kids only. If it is in your budget, you should buy for all types of people. See Table 5.1 for a sample $10,000 start-up budget for product.

Women are the largest group of buyers. Kids who typically shop with their mother are the second largest group of buyers. Men are the third largest group of buyers. Men make last minute purchases because they do not care as much as women do about what they are wearing or the cost. The smaller categories by age and gender, like tweens, teens, toddlers and plus size usually depend on much of those products you buy. If you buy these smaller categories, expect fewer customers to buy because you lack the selection they want. It is hard to please everyone, but try your best to start with the main categories, women, kids and men.

Table 5.1 Sample $10,000 Budget

General Costume Store		
Women	40%	$4000
Children	25%	$2500
Men	15%	$1500
Accessories	20%	$2000
Sexy Costume Store		
Women	65%	$6500
Men	5%	$500
Accessories	30%	$3000

When purchasing costumes, you will need to use your knowledge of pop culture to inform your buying decisions. So you will need to know about upcoming blockbuster movies, television shows and music. Blockbusters movies create a buzz around both licensed and unlicensed characters. Licensed costumes are the official manufacturers of a brand, like Disney, Marvel Comics or Nickelodeon. Unlicensed characters are generic, like pirates, vampires, witches and can include costumes that are similar to popular movies without licensing agreements. These are known as knock off licensed goods and the manufacturer will change the color or overall look so as not to infringe on the official product. For example, Pirates of the Caribbean popularized pirates each year, even though it is both a licensed and a non-licensed character. Following top music stars like Lady Gaga or Katy Perry will also give you an idea of the latest hair and fashion trends for costumes. Popular television shows offer great ideas for costumes, especially as television shows tend to stay popular for more than one Halloween season.

TIP BOX: Stay abreast of the top trashy and classy pop culture trends by following me on Twitter @99costumeideas and my Facebook Fan Page, 99 Costume Ideas. If you need content for your social media sites, you can always repost and share my content from contests.

Remember that Halloween always lags two to three years behind fashion trends. So it allows for plenty of time for you to catch up on the latest looks. The best manufacturers change traditional designs, like a pirate or witch to match the fashion trends and popular colors. You do not need to know all the fashion trends to understand Halloween costume trends, but it does help when you recognize a top selling costume does not stay popular because you keep buying the same thing. Refresh your costume purchases every three to four years, even if it is a top seller. Be open to buying new designs in the same genres to stay close to fashion trends.

Color is another important feature for costumes. Colors of costumes need to be both fashionable and reminiscent of the character, especially if the character is historic. Each year certain colors become popular and they are used in costumes. For example, 80s fashion came back into style after 2008 and bands like LMFAO sported leopard prints and Vans tennis shoes without laces. Light powder blue, fuchsia, and leopard-print were common in the 80s and came back in style.

 As a buyer, be aware costumes are manufactured to be used one day. So, not all garments are good quality. Some manufacturers cut corners to make a costume as inexpensive as possible. Most mass market costumes are made from polyesters and synthetic fabrics. Many times an image looks better than the actual costume. If you have the chance to get a sample of a costume, be sure that what you are buying looks like the picture. No matter how cheap a costume is sold, if it rips, customers are unhappy. Do not always buy the cheapest product because the quality control and final product tends to be exactly what you are paying for. Look for quality that will ensure the fewest returns and happiest customers.

After you assess the quality and understand trends, the next task is to buy costumes from the manufacturer. Once you receive the catalogs and top selling list from each manufacturer, physically layout the images by category and genre; such as all pirate costumes together or all vampires costumes together. You should plan to buy variations of color, price and design features of the same themed costumes. Mix up the number of long skirts, short dresses, pants and shorts while keeping your allotted budget in mind. As you look at the images, imagine them on your store walls or online store and decide if the costumes you have selected fit your vision of the store. Do the costumes you have in mind met your store needs or are you just interested in some of the costumes because they are top sellers? Then decide what is missing from your store. Buy more of what you need even if they are not bestselling items. A list of common genres that you can use to decide how to diversify your inventory is available in Table 5.2.

Table 5.2

Genres of Costumes			
Pirates	Vampires	Witches	Roman
Greek	Medieval	Angels and Devils	Victorian
Viking	Western	Indians	Egyptian
Fairy Tale	Animals	Pre-historic	Religious
Gothic	Circus	Superheroes	Skeletons
Ghosts	Mummies	1920s	1950s
1960s	1970s	1980s	1990s
Cops and robbers	Doctors and Nurses	Teachers	School Uniforms
Firefighters	Sailors	Pilots	Army
Licensed Costumes	Sports	Sexy Costumes	

BUYING ACCESSORIES

Similar to buying costumes, accessories require buying according to genre category and matching costumes. Accessories are wigs, weapons, special effects and any separate product that can be worn or used on the body.

This is where you can "super-size" a costume sale by having a customer buy the matching wig, shoes and wand with her fairy outfit. The average mark up on accessories is between 200-400% above the wholesale price.

Purchase most accessories from the manufacturers you are buying costumes from, to keep the total number of vendors manageable. Save between 20-30% of your costume budget for accessories. Buy more accessories for women and kids because they are more likely to spend extra money on those items. Match accessories with costumes and find general appeal accessories for different costumes. For example, a blond long wig could go with many different looks, like Alice in Wonderland, Tinkerbelle, Viking and a 1970's hippie. More specialized accessories are items that go only with a few specific costumes, like a cigarette holder from the 1920's or a machine gun for a 1950's gangsters. These are accessories that go with a specific genre, so you can decide if you need it after you start up your store.

The quality of accessories varies, especially with wigs. Synthetic wigs are weaved onto a wig cap and the less hair you weave, the less expensive the cost. Many cheap wigs made with poor quality hair fibers are in the market. The best way to assess the wig quality is to see it out of the package and to feel the hair. Also, look underneath to see how thin or thick the hair is in the wig cap. Most of the other accessories, like weapons and make-up vary in quality and I recommend seeing the product before you purchase it. Always get a feel and compare the quality at different prices.

BUYING DECORATIONS

Halloween decorations are for home or office use. Decorations are usually larger than life size tombstones, spiders, skeletons and can even include life size pirate ships and many more ideas. Decorations come in many sizes, however you will want to keep the size of decorations smaller based on your store size. It is more fun to enjoy larger than life decorations, but it does not usually mean more money. Buy décor and decorations like buying costumes. It must fit into a smaller area of your store of warehouse. Buying decorations should be limited to high volume items with a unique function. Night clubs, restaurants and home Halloween decorators love buying these products. Decorations are a must for your own office, warehouse and store. This will create the right atmosphere for you, your staff and customers.

HOW MUCH TO BUY

If you have an online store, you should spend 75% of your total budget for your business on costumes. The other 25% is for your overhead, such as buying packing tape, boxes and shipping labels. An online store is a lean operation to start, so keep all expenses to a minimum.

When buying for a temporary store or year-round store, you should spend 50% of your total budget on costumes. The other 50% is for your overhead, such as rent, employees and utilities. Since the products being merchandised need to be displayed on the floor, you need a formula to determine how much space you will need. This is a general estimate for product.

$ per Square Foot (in wholesale $ for retail space only)	Fill-rate of Product in the Retail Store Space	EXAMPLE: 500 Square Foot Store	EXAMPLE: 4000 Square Foot Store
$12 to $16	Total budget for all products. Completely filled shelves	$6000 to $8000	$48000 to $64000
$8 to $11	Medium filled shelves	$4000 to $5500	$32000 to $44000
$4 to $7	Lightly filled shelves	$2000 to $3500	$16000 to $28000
$1 to $3	Sampling a product for store	$500 to $1500	$4000 to $12000

This estimator for the amount of product, costumes, wigs, accessories and décor, by square foot is based on the total retail space for customers. It includes the racks for all products, dressing rooms, aisles, cash registers, staircases and display space. It does not include storage, stock area, break rooms, warehouse or bathrooms. Total the amount of retail space for customers and multiply it by $12 to $16 to find your total budget. This is the starting amount of money you need to fill out the store with product. When you look at each manufacturer and try to decide how much to spend with each company, you can use the $8 to $11, $4 to $7 and $1 to $3 ranges to decide the budget amount you will commit.

At $12 to $16 per square foot, this would be the total budget and it could also be the total amount of money you could spend with one manufacturer for their product. I wouldn't buy only one company to fill out your store, but if you wanted to spend it only on one company, you have a dollar amount.

At $8 to $11 per square foot, it would cover a medium amount of your shelves, between 45%-65% of the retail space. This could be your budget to spend on a majority of a manufacturer's product. This leaves in your budget to spend it on other manufacturers.

At $4 to $7 per square foot, this would cover a light amount of your shelves, between 25%-40% of the retail space. This could be your budget if you want to spend a smaller amount of money on a manufacturer's product line, while having enough to give customers a variety.

At $1 to $3 per square foot, it is a sample of how a product line will do in your store. If you like a company's product but are not sure it fits with the rest of what you bought or you are testing new products, this is about how much you want to spend.

This estimator for the budget on product and how to break down the budget for each manufacturer is to fill the retail store space. You should always buy enough to fill your shelves and have stock to replace what is selling. Replacement stock is not calculated in this estimator, because you determine how much or little you will purchase during the Halloween season.

CHAPTER 5: BUYING LOGISTICS

In the Halloween industry, there are numerous suppliers, distributors and manufacturers eager for your business. Each company has their own ordering, shipping and payment methods. Negotiating the costs associated with each of these aspects of a purchase order is a part of doing business. Once you have ordered and received costumes and accessories for your store, effectively managing what you have and what you are selling is crucial to success.

ORDERING

The Halloween industry prefers to receive your order as early in the year as possible, between January and March. So as soon as you have decided on everything that you want to buy you will be ready to place your first Purchase Order (PO).

Even though there are benefits to placing your order in the first few months of the calendar year, you should be sure about the products you want. Changes to your order are always allowed, but every change increases the chance of mistakes. When you must change your order, always ask for an order confirmation of the changes for your records.

If you are new at selling Halloween, you may want to buy only a few products to see how well they sell and then submit more POs as Halloween approaches. But keep in mind that there is a trade-off to this approach. Since most Halloween orders are placed between January and March, the items you are most interested in ordering later may not be available.

SHIPPING

When placing your order, inform your supplier when to start shipping your products and when to cancel shipping for items not in stock. A start ship date is followed by a cancel ship date. The cancel ship date is the last day you will allow a backorder to arrive before a purchase order (PO) is canceled. In the Halloween industry, most companies need a cancel ship date, even if you are willing to take goods anytime in the future.

Shipments vary by size and weight, which determines the method of transportation. In the US, smaller shipments under one pallet go by UPS or FedEx. A pallet is a flat wooden structure that is usually 4 feet by 4 feet wooden structure used to transport boxes by piling them on top. The wooden structure allows a fork lift to move it easily. The size of the pallet can vary slightly based on how it is being shipped. When shipments are larger than one pallet and less than a 20 or 40 foot container, the shipment can go by truck across country or by less-than-a-load (LTL) sea freight to international destinations. Truck shipments usually take 5-6 days from coast to coast in the US. When you are shipping in larger quantities, you should compare the cost of shipping for local trucking companies.

UPS and FedEx by ground are relatively cheap. In the US, UPS or FedEx is about 6-9% of the invoice for ground service. Faster delivery service by UPS or FedEx-1-Day, 2-Day or 3-Day costs more. To get a large shipment rushed, you would need to use air freight.

Air freight is offered by UPS and FedEx internationally. For international orders, the cost is always higher for air freight. The United States Postal Service (USPS) also delivers internationally. International shipments become more expensive when packages are air shipped or rushed.

If you are importing goods from another country, they must go through customs. Large shipments need a freight forwarder, a private company that specializes in shipping goods internationally, to get product into a country. They are familiar with customs and duties. There are hundreds of freight forwarding companies in each country, so shop for the best rate. If you are importing product from another country, get the dimensions, weight and the type of goods for a shipping quote. Compare quotes and always bargain for a better price.

BACKORDERS

In my work with new entrepreneurs in the Halloween industry, I have learned that backorders seem more complicating than they are. When you place an order with a Halloween company, they often do not have everything in stock. The product they do not have in stock is called a backorder. For example, if you order 100 costumes from a company and they only have 75 costumes available to ship, the remaining 25 costumes are called backordered product. Some companies have a live inventory system where you can monitor the stock levels and decide what to buy based on availability.

You can also ask when your backordered items will be in stock. Some companies are transparent with their product inventory and others are not as organized, so they are not always accurate with their inventory. If you need the product right away, and they are out of stock, you may have to buy a similar product from a different company. If you no longer want to receive a backorder, you simply tell the company you want to cancel the backorder.

Backorders is a key part of getting more of your order fulfilled if they can be delivered in time for the Halloween season. Choosing a cancel ship date for backorders will ensure you won't get charged for product shipped after a time you consider to be too late. For online stores, the best cancel ship date for Halloween is between September 15 and October 1, so you can have time to upload the image and description onto your website. For temporary stores and year round stores, the best cancel ship date is between October 1 and October 10, because you will get more customers shopping until the day before Halloween.

The Halloween industry has built itself around a projected demand for October 31, rather than for year round sales or international sales trends. The reason is because Halloween suppliers sell for the biggest time of year, not necessarily to have stock year round.

That means when you have a backorder after Halloween, it will not likely be fulfilled since the industry builds it inventory for the following year. Manufacturing companies receive new product on a rolling basis between March and August for Halloween. They can often get early shipments that run out and later shipments that are too late to sell for Halloween.

PAYMENTS

Paying for costumes is easy. You can wire transfer the money right away or pay by credit card. Most companies love to be paid in advance or when your order is being shipped. However, manufacturers have traditionally offered credit terms to customers through a factored bank. Factoring banks allow you to put business assets as collateral for a line of credit used to place a PO. If you have an established company with assets, then you can apply to factor with a bank. That means if you cannot pay, they go after your assets and the company you purchased goods from gets paid. The best payment term is called "Halloween dating." This means you can use your line of credit to buy costumes throughout the year and pay all bills by November 1, the day after Halloween. This is the most desirable payment term in the US. Other credit terms are Net 30, Net 60 and Net 90, in which you are expected to pay within the specific number of days (30, 60 or 90) after the invoice. Those terms are usually given for year round orders which are more often negotiable.

Payment terms vary with each manufacturing company. If you are not getting a line of credit with a factored bank, manufacturing companies ask for asset collateral, like a personal guarantee to show faith in paying on time. Manufacturers do offer in-house terms not financed by a bank. However, it is risky for manufacturing companies to offer payment terms since they risk not getting paid if a customer buys product and cannot pay. It helps to build a history of paying on time, then they feel more comfortable giving payment terms.

Here are a few good questions to ask to see if you likely qualify for payment terms:

- **Can I get Halloween Dating for my order?**
- **Can I pay a small percentage upon shipping and pay the rest of my invoices on November 1? For example, ask if you can pay 50% now and 50% on November 1.**
- **Do you offer better terms if I buy more? If so, how much do I need to purchase?**
- **Can I get Net 30/60/90 terms or Halloween Dating if I use a credit card or post-dated check as collateral? Remember, NET 30/60/90 is the number of days after you have been invoiced**

that you must pay your bills. For example, Net 30 means the payment is due 30 days after the invoice is issued.

All these questions should help you understand in-house payment systems and if you have room to negotiate with a particular company. Remember if they offer you any payment terms, you need to pay on time and build a good relationship with your suppliers. If you pay late or you do not have the money, you will not get terms in the future. Do not risk your reputation or your business. There are very few industries that will offer these payment terms to a new customer, so treat it like a gift.

Do not only buy costumes from companies that offer you payment terms. That would be financially unwise. You should buy product you need for your store from as many manufacturers as needed. After all, the rest of your competitors will be getting similar terms and they will carry much of the same products. There will be a lot of competition for those products because it was so easy to obtain them without payment. Therefore, increased competition for the same item will mean lower profit margins for everyone. Create a balance between product bought from costume companies that have what you need to succeed and offer payment terms.

INVENTORY MANAGEMENT

Inventory management is often an afterthought when you start with a small budget. If you are only selling online through already established retailers such as eBay, you can use the tracking systems for purchases (sales history) available on their websites or Paypal to track your progress. For physical stores, you must implement a point of sales system from the start. [Note: Several Point of Sales systems were identified in chapter 2] It will make doing business easier to manage for you and your accountant.

Managing inventory effectively is required in order to adequately fulfill sales in the moment. The more data you have on what you have, the better equipped you are to sell it. Better yet, the more data you have on what is out of stock and what is expected to be delivered, the more sales you will be able to make. When product comes in it is counted and when product is sold it is subtracted. If things are damaged or returned, it is marked in the system. Each day the computer takes accounts for all transactions. You can run daily reports to monitor sales by genre, age, cost or any other parameter you set up. Point of Sale analyses can inform you and your staff of top sellers, slow sellers and the ideal price point for your product. You can experiment with prices to see the effect of price changes on sales. This is why I always advocate for a Point of Sale system.

STAFF

If you have are starting an online store and you have a day job, you should consider hiring at least one temporary staff to help out with orders during the height of the Halloween season. In brick and mortar stores you will need a variety of staff to carry out the many duties involved in day to day operations. You will need back stock, floor, register, dressing room and security staff members.

The back stock staff will receive shipments and count and shelve product on the store floor. Back stock staff will have the responsibility of organizing products in the stock area so they are easy to find. This will allow product to be replaced on the store floor as quickly as possible. These staff members will also need to be trained in the use of the Point of Sale (POS) inventory system you will be using.

The floor staff will help customers try on costumes, find the products they need and keep the merchandise organized so that the store is neat and presentable at all times. These staff members should have good customer service and selling skills. For example, they will need to help customers to make decisions about purchases when they are unsure of what to buy or when an item they want is out of stock.

The Register staff members will be responsible for helping customers to checkout and handle returns. They will be handling cash and need to have a basic level of math competency. It is especially important to have trustworthy staff members in this position. You will also need to have dressing room staff to keep the areas clean and address the needs of the customers. To decrease employee and customer theft and minimize chaos among customers in dressing room and lines during busy periods, you will also need to hire security staff.

Even though you should hire staff for specific positions it is recommended that the entire staff be provided with basic training in all job responsibilities so they can be flexible and help out as needed.

TIP BOX: Some employees do not take the job as seriously as others. However, reminding them of the potential to work with them during the off season or the following year may increase their motivation. Also, offer the best staff the chance to be a part of the planning committee for next year's theme and decoration. Let them contribute to the creativity.

CHAPTER 6: MERCHANDISING & PRICING

MERCHANDISING

Well executed merchandising is crucial to the success of any Halloween business. You want to make sure that you make your online or brick and mortar store as visually appealing and motivates the browser to make a purchase. You also want to make sure that your costumes and accessories are easy to find and customers can learn more about the product on your website or in the store. Great merchandised stores make it easy to buy with minimal or no assistance from staff.

ONLINE MERCHANDISING

Online merchandising should be designed to create a pleasurable shopping experience and up-sell customers into buying more products. To be successful, merchandise should be organized so that it is easy for the potential customer to find what they are looking for. Think about your customer and what they will come to your site to do. Will they come to browse, compare, get ideas or make a purchase? Do they need advice or want access to customer service? Since most customers will be coming to your website for multiple reasons, you want to try to meet as many needs of their needs as possible. Of course you cannot be everything to everyone but try to meet the needs of your select customer base as much as possible.

 I suggest you cross-categorize merchandise to address the most common needs of online shoppers. Allow customers to browse the same products in many different categories: costume genre or theme; brand name; occasion or special event; browse by color; best deals and bestsellers. These are the minimum categories you should have for your website.

Once a customer creates a custom search, they should land on a category page or be shown a product listing page, depending on how narrow the search is.

TIP BOX: Check out

http://www.thehalloweenbusiness.com/book/categorysearch for an example of how to organize the category pages and searches.

For category pages create a banner to the major search categories. If a customer wants to look at 1920's costumes, from a list of banners that show all categories, then it can be found on the main category page. As a customer narrows the search, the banner page leads them to a list of costume images. This list of costume images is the product listing page. The listing page shows enough of each costume to allow shoppers to browse the searched and narrow the list to 40-80 at a time. The category page shows them a banner with popular costume images for each category and then shows a listing of costumes in that category. Lastly, the product page itself is where a single product is displayed. This topic is discussed in more detail in the marketing section of this book.

TEMPORARY AND YEAR ROUND STORE MERCHANDISING

Merchandising for a physical store location involves creating a shopping experience for customers that will get them into the spirit of Halloween and displaying products so they are attractive to shoppers and easy to find. The best merchandised spaces are clean and easy to navigate and set up to encourage shoppers to buy more than they intended. A store that has a lot of variety in product, like laughing pumpkins, fake blood, wigs, costumes and life size tombstones will look cluttered if you do not keep it organized. The Apple stores are a great example of an optimally merchandised store. Everything is organized and clean, making for a high end shopping experience. If a customer comes into your Halloween store only wanting to purchase a blond wig but ends up buying a costume, matching shoes and leggings, then you will know that you and your staff have created the optimal shopping experience.

To merchandise the store space there are four areas to focus on:

1. Front display or window display

2. Aisle end caps

3. Aisles, with costumes and accessories

4. Décor and small items.

These major areas to merchandise will help drive sales and are the main visual store features.

Front Display or Window Display

The visual shopping experience starts with the front window or front display. This is the first impression people get about the store from outside. The first impression determines if a shopper wants to go in or just look from the outside. Make the front display amazing and entice people to want to see more inside. Create a scene with costumes, props and décor. It can be scary, sexy, weird, funny or creepy. For example a group of clowns getting out of a VW bug with a sinister face, will attract people to look at the details and action. Another example is creating a scene with aliens landing from a space ship and abducting humans for experiments. The scene should be movie set quality with plenty of small details so it holds the attention of window shoppers. If you display any costumes on mannequins, always be sure you stock those items in your store. Store displays make it easy for shoppers to imagine themselves in a costume.

Aisle End Caps

The end of the aisle is referred to as the end cap. Once you have enticed shoppers into the store, continue the high quality displays on the end of each aisle. This is where shoppers can glance down the end caps to see suggestions on costume themes. It is the same as the grocery store, the end caps are new products or products on sale. The end cap is attention grabbing and helps sell a group of related products.

Use the end cap space to introduce the category theme in the aisle and to sell a complete set for a single costume idea. For example, create a sexy costume combination with a mannequin wearing a wig, shoes, leggings and the make-up kit on the end cap for women's costumes. On the end cap, sell the product pictured with all the accessories, so shoppers already have everything in front of them. An example of a sexy costume combination would be a zombie woman eating a brain in a sexy nurse outfit, with a two-colored wig, the shoes, fake blood and make-up to look dead.

Aisle with Costumes and Accessories
The organization of each aisle is crucial for sales. Customers spend considerable time within the aisles looking for their ideal costume. The easier it is for a customer to see a costume, the easier it is for them to buy it. Overall store organization should be based on large categories by gender, age and size. The most common categories are: Women, Men, Girls, Boys, Plus size, teen, infant and toddler. The merchandise in the aisles should reflect this organization in smaller theme categories and sections. For example if you stock vampire related costumes you would want to put them all in one aisle. Within the aisle, the specific vampire related accessories such as fangs and white make-up should be displayed together in a separate section, nearby.

Once the costumes are organized in the aisles, you can decide to keep accessories separate or mixed in with the costumes. If you mix accessories with the costumes, you will sell more. Having the accessories for a complete costume in the same place makes it more convenient for customers and saves them time.

While displaying accessories with costumes increases sales, it also takes a lot more room to display and often it is still necessary to set up a separate section for the same accessories to be displayed. An alternative suggestion is to display only wigs with costumes and display all other accessories together in a separate section of the store.

Décor and Small Accessories

Halloween decorations or décor are items such as tombstones, life size zombies, scene props and fake pumpkins. If you carry décor in your store you always want to have it on display. Small accessories can be items like key chains with skulls, vampire teeth or Halloween candy. These smaller and often low cost items are what my mom calls "impulse buys."

Merchandising large and small items is tricky and they are usually too large to display all of them or too small to be easily found on a shelf. Décor is large and it not easy to show customers the entire set. Décor are items that decorate a space and if you carry décor, always leave out a few items for display. People want to know how it works. For small items, merchandise them by the check-out register and extending back into area where the check-out line begins. These smaller items are only a few more dollars and people often play with them while they wait in line.

TIP BOX: Set up one dressing room for every 800 square feet of retail space. Also, limit the number of costumes to three per customer. If possible, give the customer only the main pants, shirt, skirts or dress to try on. Leave the accessories with a staff so they are not lost or stolen.

PRICING

Price is the easiest competitive edge to offer customers. The traditional mark up on costumes-keystone pricing-is double the wholesale cost. Today, keystone pricing is merely a suggestion. As a result of the Internet there is more competition in costume availability and pricing. But remember, there is a customer at every price point and being the cheapest is not the most attractive incentive. The goal is to stay within the competition with your prices while still maintaining a profit. Similarly, prices at temporary and year round stores are regulated by the atmosphere of the store and the socioeconomic status of the community. Regardless of competition, your prices and store will attract the type of customer you need.

ONLINE PRICING

Pricing online is usually lower than keystone pricing, double the wholesale cost. Usually, the online store price is between 150% and 180% of the wholesale price. Do not start with extremely low prices just to make a few extra dollars. Instead, find out what other retailers are charging and find a comfortable middle ground. With Amazon and eBay, it is easy to price compare items. For your own website, Google is making it easier to price compare with their comparison shopping engine (CSE) *Google Shopping*. Keep in mind that *Google Shopping* and all other CSEs make it easy for retailers and customers to compare prices. The ability for customers to comparison shop online is the primary reason that the cost of costume has dropped.

You can legitimately make extra money with the cost of shipping. Shipping costs vary depending on the weight of the package and the location it is being shipped to. If you charge a flat rate for domestic shipping, you should always have a cushion for your expenses. Shipping internationally by flat rate is also a way to collect an extra cushion for your expenses.

Table 6.1

Mark-Up and Shipping Example		Domestic Shipping $8 (Recommended Charge)	Domestic Shipping $5 (actual cost)
Wholesale Price	$15		
150% of wholesale price	$22.50	$30.50	$27.50
180% of wholesale price (recommended price)	$27.00	$35.00	$32.00
200% of wholesale Price (Keystone Price)	$30.00	$38.00	$35.00

If you use the recommended 180% of the wholesale price of $27 you will be in the middle of your competitors. But when you add the $8 shipping charge, the total cost is $35. Your profit is $12 + $3 = $15 and total cost will be the same as the retailer who uses the keystone price and charges $5 for shipping. This is an effective way to stay competitive.

TEMPORARY STORE PRICING

Temporary stores usually have less emphasis on décor and make it a goal to sell merchandise at keystone prices. Product is only discounted during promotions or after Halloween only to deplete inventory. Temporary stores should start between keystone pricing and 250% of the wholesale prices. But be willing to be flexible and start at a lower price depending on the income levels of customers, overhead costs and nearby competition. This gives you room to lower costs or understand the customer's willingness to pay for the shopping experience. You should consider price matching if customers find the same costume advertised by a competitor.

YEAR ROUND PRICING

Pricing at year round stores should start at keystone pricing. But if set your store up like a high-end boutique, or an ultimate shopping experience you will be able to charge more for products. Ideal locations for these types of Year-Round stores are in higher socioeconomic neighborhoods. In the United States real estate in these areas are expensive, however in the expanding international Halloween market these types of stores are less expensive to set up.

OTHER PRICING STRATEGIES

Cross-selling, up-selling and volume discounting are also great ways to increase the sale before a shopper pays. Cross-selling involves including suggestions of other similar items to buy such as "customers who bought this also bought this." Showing customers accessories, weapons, wigs and shoes that complement a costume would be up-selling. Volume discounting refers to offering a discount when customers' purchases exceed a certain dollar amount or number of items. An example of a volume discount would be offering fee shipping on orders above $75. Another example of volume discounting would be "buy two wigs you get a third one free."

CHAPTER 7-OPERATIONS

Once the store is set up, the staff is trained, the product is merchandised and the marketing is in place, the next big step is opening to the public. When your doors open, you are officially in business. That is both a rush of excitement and stressful as you wait for customers to find you.

CUSTOMER SERVICE

The customer experience in your store or on your website is the key ingredient for getting return customers and strong word of mouth sales. So you should consider your customers' experiences in every aspect of your store.

For online stores, you have fewer aspects of the customer experience to handle but the ways in which you may need to provide excellent customer service may be more crucial since you will not have face to face contact. For online stores, you should set up a live chat, a phone line and quick response to email particularly in the month of October. If you have a full time job, you should hire at least one additional employee to assist with these tasks as well as taking orders and shipping.

For brick and mortar stores, in the early days of opening, offer customers a reason to buy early by giving them a discount coupon usable within the next week. A few examples of coupons you could offer a percentage off of the retail price or a free consult with a Halloween make-up artist.

HOURS OF OPERATION

Be sure your hours of operation are clearly on the door, so when customers stop by when you are closed they will know when to return. It is recommended that you start with the following hours of operation:

Monday through Friday 10 AM-10 PM

Saturday and Sunday   8 AM-11PM

Start with these hours for staffing, but feel free to change them according to the customer traffic. Customers will shop until hours before a Halloween party, so keep the doors open all night on October 31.

IN STORE RETURNS

Most Halloween stores have a "No Returns" policy. It is a common practice for customers to wear a costume to a party and then return it for a refund. But some returns should be considered if a costume is labeled the wrong size, is damaged or an accessory is missing. One challenge with damage returns is you do not know if the damage occurred from the manufacturer or if the costumer wore it and damaged it. A return can be for money back or exchange only. You can decide what you want your return policy to be. What's most important is that your return policy is clear about the type of returns you will accept and the conditions under which you will accept them.

A common way to prevent returns after Halloween is to have a no refund policy two weeks before Halloween. This will ensure that all sales are final the busiest days of October. Always weigh the cost of not returning a costume because of your policy and the cost of an unhappy customer. Customers are your best marketing tool and with so many websites available for posting complaints about your customer service, you want to always be mindful of the benefits of fewer negative reviews and increasing positive reviews.

TIP BOX: To set up a good flow of customer traffic and decrease theft, place all registers in the front of the store.

HIGH TRAFFIC

In a brick and mortar store you will be very busy once the Halloween season begins. During the last two weeks before Halloween, crowd control will be an issue. Many people will want to get their costumes, so organizing the number of people in the store and quickly getting them checked out will require extra effort from all staff members. Always keep in mind that even if it is the evening of Halloween, the most important things from a shoppers' perspective is the ability to find what they want, getting assistance from staff as needed and enjoying the store experience.

Be sure to have plenty of floor staff helping customers find product and get into the dressing rooms, refolding product and keeping the aisles clear. Shoppers will be less inclined to make purchases if they find the store to be disorganized or not well stocked.
Arrange to have as many staff members working the store and to stay open long enough to see the last person through the line. You will need to make sure you have a few extra well trained staff as door greeters and floaters who can pitch in and help out with almost any job functions. Every evening after the store closes, clean and tidy the space for tomorrow. Pack all costumes for the next day and organize the merchandise.

Your security staff will also be crucial during this high traffic period. Employee theft is common for temporary stores or warehouses because it is easier to get away with stealing, especially if they know the job is only going to last a few weeks. Also, due to the high volume activity, it will be necessary to have security staff check customers' purses and bags being brought into the store to minimize theft.

TIP BOX: If you run low on costumes close to Halloween and cannot get more, you can always put the party merchandise on display. It is better to have full shelves than bare shelves. An empty store close to Halloween will look like it is going out of business, so keep it looking full and neat.

LONG LINES

Try to minimize the number of customers wanting to play dress-up with merchandise and keep the lines in front of the store, in dressing rooms and cash registers moving.

If you have a long line outside, keep shoppers entertained with TV, a clown making animal balloons or a staff employee scaring kids and giving out candy. As customers look for what they want, a line will begin to form outside of the dressing rooms. Be sure they do not look overly long or daunting because people will give up shopping in your store if they see a long line. Once a customer is inside the store and they see long lines by the registers, they may decide they do not want to shop. Train the staff to ask if they need help and that the line moves quickly.

For the last few days before Halloween, have the security guard manage the maximum number of shoppers in the store, the line outside and the line inside at the dressing rooms and checkout line. A security guard can also help to minimize the chaotic interactions between customers who may grow impatient while waiting to enter the store.

TRYING ON COSTUMES

When a customer wants to try on a costume, only allow them to try on the main costume elements from the outfit; the dress, skirt, blouse, the pants or shirt. Keep the rest of the costume pieces with a staff member nearby the dressing room area. This will prevent customers from stealing whole or partial costumes. Often customers will steal a nice pair of leggings or a hat while they are in the dressing room, and then leave the rest of the costume for the staff to fold and search for missing pieces. The dressing room staff needs to be the most organized when there is a crowd. They will be required to move people through the line quickly while folding and repackaging the costumes to be sold to other customers. If the costumes are not put back out on the retail shelves, then it could mean lost sales because the sizes or the styles were not available.

TIP BOX: Minimize customers trying on costumes in the aisles because it stretches the fabric over their clothes. It could damage the costume. Many times this happens when they do not want to wait in the dressing room line.

END OF SEASON

After Halloween, clean up the space, pack the remaining inventory and reward yourself and your staff for the two months of hard work with a farewell costume party. If you can, rent out a restaurant or bar space for the party. It's is a great to say "thank you" to staff. If the season was not as lucrative, you might choose to celebrate in the empty store space before the lease expires.

A staff party can be just as much for you as it is for your staff, no matter how well you know your staff. They want to feel as if they put in extra hours and hard work towards an opportunity to have fun. Many temporary store workers may not come back to work for you again if they find permanent jobs or you did not want to ask them back next year. It is all okay. This is your chance to celebrate and seize the moment. This is also a chance for you to relax and not be in a work environment with your staff so you can get to know them, see them in a social setting and really identify the employees you would like to ask back the next year. It is always nice to open the party up to their family and close friends. You only get a maximum of two months with your staff, in a high pressure and intense work environment, so you might see your staff differently when you see them interact with people that know them well. They might also choose to bring someone to the party who may be worth hiring next season.

CHAPTER 8: PROMOTING YOUR BUSINESS

This chapter is a big one. It describes Branding, Marketing and Advertising. These are the most important parts of business. Branding is the image and feel of you company to your customers and staff. Marketing is a way of educating, informing and explaining your business to the world. Advertising is the method of getting your company, your voice and your product or service out to the world. Branding establishes who you are in the world, so you can market the products or services you have by finding places to post or show what you have advertised. All three of these are related to each other.

BRANDING

Branding is your logo, colors, purpose and philosophy that create the look and feel of your company. Your brand is easiest explained in a company manifesto, which explains what you do and why you do it. Developing a brand is a skill that corporations do so the name conjures up certain images without seeing the product, like Coke or Pepsi. The next generation of buyers and entrepreneurs want to quickly understand who you are. It is the age of transparent selling and soon cheap prices will not be the only motivation to buy from you. Your manifesto helps you brand be more than cheap products. You do not have to be the Coke or Pepsi in the Halloween world, but you do want to have the basics. Create a logo with colors that inspire the type of customer you want to attract.

Develop a tagline to go with your branded logo. It should be a short sentence or phrase. Your tagline is how you will describe yourself when people ask what you do or what your company is about. Here is a good example of a tagline for a company, called Costume Panda, "We are not your typical black and white affair. We dress you for any occasion." This is the line Costume Panda uses in all advertisements. Costume Panda should keep this tagline unless their business objectives change.

TIP BOX: Check out my manifesto on TheHalloweenBusiness.com to see how I explain my purpose.

Your tagline should be humorous. This is the costume business, there is nothing more fun than tongue and cheek punches. I encourage you to brand your humor as your business. It will attract customers who enjoy buying from a company that can laugh at themselves.

MARKETING

Attracting customers is where marketing enters the picture. Marketing is the way to be seen and heard by the public. Marketing plans includes developing social media, advertising in print and digitally and create word-of-mouth recommendations. Your website is a

great marketing tool for customers looking for costumes or Halloween products. To start marketing, always have a website and word-of-mouth because they are simple and the most effective. Social Media is all the rage to use as a marketing tool because you can engage with many different groups and target the marketing message depending on what you want them to buy.
Additionally, your company can fragment your marketing into defined demographics. For example, a marketing campaign to attract more women buyers or a marketing campaign for busy professionals.

ADVERTISING

Advertising is the vehicle to get your message out to the masses. You can choose to print fliers, create a Facebook flier and pay Google to put your paid advertisement higher in searches online. Those places are called ad space but the message written for each space is different, according to the type of person who reads it. Advertising can be free or paid. With the power of the internet, it is important to put more advertisements online than in print.

PROMOTIONAL MARKETING STRATEGIES

Traditional promotional marketing is a combination of old fashioned advertising and guerilla marketing methods to get the word out about your store. The goal of promotional marketing is to direct more traffic to your store. This can include a discount coupon or a limited time only offer to create urgency in visiting your store. Some old fashioned advertising methods are local newspapers, local TV ads, mailers to nearby residents and handouts to people and cars at large events. When customers buy from you in the store, always give them a discount coupon for a future visit or have them give it to a friend to buy a costume. Guerilla marketing includes sign twirlers, impersonators and flash mobs, which all should be recorded and used as YouTube videos advertising your store.

For brick and mortar stores, traditional marketing strategies can enhance your online marketing strategies but will not be sufficient to sustain your business. There are two types of promotional market strategies that I recommend to add to your online marketing, advertising street teams and print advertisements.

ADVERTISING STREET TEAM

A street team creates human to human contact with people they encounter in high traffic areas to promote your business. For example in Las Vegas, there are dozens of promoters on the strip passing out cards for clubs and discount shows. The best way to get people to take a flier from a street team person is have them dressed in a costume.

I recommend hiring an impersonator or actor to dress up as Captain Jack Sparrow or Snow White to pass out fliers at local hot spots. Have these impersonators say fun lines like, "Tell them Captain Jack Sparrow sent you" or "This is the poisonous apple that you must bring with you for a 10% discount." If people who see them want to take a photo with the impersonators, have the impersonator hold up a small sign advertising your store logo and website. The impersonator could invite them to post the photo to their Social Media site and tag your store in it in exchange for an entry into a contest to win a costume make over for Halloween or a discount on their purchase. This is a way to ensure you get free publicity from users who post to your page. Record a few key lines and jokes from the impersonator and use that to create a YouTube video commercial. It is a spoof on the real person.

Another example of an advertising street team is the use of sign twirlers on the street to grab the attention of drivers waiting. A sign twirler holds a sign up and can spin it on their hands and body. People in cars watch the talented twirler tossing the sign around as they wait for the signal to change. This is great advertisement. For additional fun visibility, have the sign twirler wear a costume. Imagine having a gorilla sign twirler or an Elvis sign twirler. Make a fun promotional YouTube video of the talented twirlers and upload it to your website.

If you are located in a mall, hire a dance troupe of four to six people to wear costumes and do a choreographed dance in the busiest shopping spot. It would help if they can dance to a pop song or a remix of a few songs. This will be great for kids, teens and young adults to get into the spirit of Halloween. A great idea for a choreographed dance would be a reenactment of Michael Jackson's Thriller with a few dancers that come from a crowd like a flash mob. A flash mob dance is organized online by groups who teach each other the dance and then find a place to mob by dancing together and slowly adding in more people. Check out YouTube for some great flash mobs. It is a popular and great way to advertise your store.

PRINT ADVERTISEMENTS

With so much advertisement taking place online, paid print ads should be created when there is a clear return on the investment. A return on your investment can be tracked by using coupon codes or smart phone QR codes on the printed advertisement, so you can count the number of people using the discount. Printed materials are usually fliers, mailers, posters for public display. Have handouts designed by a professional graphic designer. Hire the graphic designer early enough so you have your advertisements, handouts and signs made in time for the start of the Halloween season. The ad should give potential customers a compelling reason to visit your store. Giving a discount or a limited offer will ensure people keep your printed material or pass it onto someone else. There should still always be a human to human connection to receive a flier. Do not leave a stack of fliers at local businesses or place them on parked cars because they are seldom found or viewed.

INTERNET MARKETING

A store website should be an extension of your store and how your store feels inside. The website should be branded to consistently share your logo colors and fonts in your store. Aside from the website marketing basics for any business, I highly recommend registering your store, even if it is for two months, with Google Maps. Go to the Google Local Business Center and register your business It takes 20 minutes and it's an easy and free form of advertising. For a new business, you'll see the changes right away. For an update to an existing business, it can take 3-4 weeks. This information will appear online and on smart phones.

CONTENT

Google is the king of searches, so create a website and content that Google likes. A good website for costumes should contain a; home page, products page, an about page, a contact us page and a shopping cart.

BLOGS

Blogging and vlogging are how the public finds and learns about new information being searched. You should blog or vlog, a video blog, to create content that will help readers you're your store and trust you as a business. Google defines a blog entry at 300-700 words. This is the ideal length for most people to read. Start by making a list of facts and stories you want people to know about costumes, parties and ideas. For example, "The top 5 ways to use your grandmother's old clothes plus a wolf mask to meet more Little Red Riding Hoods." This is a great hook for creating a couples costume or meeting a cute girl on Halloween. Also it shows creativity and people are intrigued by your list of five. Now you are building credibility and an audience who will take note of your business. This is what brand building looks like today. You are branding yourself as creative, fun and you happen to sell wolf masks and Little Red Riding Hood costumes too. You want potential customers to notice you over time. This rapport building and information you create adds value to their experience. People will find you.

Aside from product, free information and advice are what build a brand online. When you sell product, it helps if you show how your product is more fun or unique through your content, such as a blog. When people like what you have to say they will want to follow your words and work. They can follow you on Social Media sites and as a member of your email list. Building a list is valuable in two ways, creating a fan community and selling ideas and products.

Building a list is a bonus for offering good content and products. Once you have begun to gather email addresses and subscribers, create a funnel to continually distribute information to your fans and community. Email them with information, discounts, products to look out for and costume ideas. You should send a minimum of six to ten emails on a weekly basis to stay in front of your new fans. It takes a minimum of seven exposures to a brand to remember it, so use this as a start place. Beyond the first few emails, you can email them when you have new content along the way.

VIDEOS

The future of sales will be in what you show and less about what you say. YouTube is the premiere video showcase site and it is owned by Google. Create a video for your business, for your manifesto, for who you are and the advice or free information you have. For product, start by featuring the manufacturers' video to sell individual costumes. Place those videos by the photos that help sell the costume item. You may also decide to create a splash video combining individual costumes as a teaser for a costume genre or homepage. For example, the category 70s costumes, should have a landing page, where you can view all of the 70s costumes with small images. A great site to find someone to make short trailers is fiverr.com. I have had great success using this website where small services really can be done starting at $5.

Videos are useful to entertain your potential customers and show them quickly what they will find on your site. Videos should be both entertaining and informative. Additionally, those same videos will be useful on your Social Media pages, like Facebook and YouTube, to drive traffic to your website. Finally, it helps build more search engine optimization (SEO) strength to see customers coming from different websites to your homepage.

Videos are necessary for you company brand to inform online users of what you do and what makes you special. You can educate people on fashion trends, how to fit a costume with easy fixes or how to style a wig on. These unique videos can often be found by your competitors or smaller websites who want to also build useful content. For all videos you post or that you use from manufacturers, allow viewers to share this video to their own social media networks and monitor the conversations about these products. If you own the original content for a video, this is a great way to track the origination of your images and how quickly they get passed around on social media networks.

SEO

Once you have a website, you should optimize it so it can easily be found on Google, Bing, Yahoo, and other search engines. If you are searchable, then more traffic will come to your site. SEO is a basic structure of key phrases and words for your website to gain recognition on these search engines. When customers search for costume names or genres, like "80s costumes" or "Sexy Halloween costumes for men" then those words should appear on your site as to connect a search to your website. Your website should have phrases and words that help a search engine recognize what your site offers, through the written content and the backlinks. A backlink is the information that search engines see when they catalog the words from you site. The easier it is to find your information and the longer the information exists on the internet, the better it looks to SEO programs. You can pay a web developer or a freelance person to SEO your website. If you use WordPress for your website, and want to try search engine optimizing your website yourself, Yoast (http://yoast.com/) would be the best program to use.

ONLINE AFFLIATE MARKETING

Online affiliate marketing is a type of performance-based marketing in which a business rewards one or more affiliates for each customer brought by the affiliate's own marketing efforts. In the simplest form, affiliate marketing has four core players: the merchant-your online business brand; the network-the community or group targeted to buy costumes; the publisher-the person or organization that will drive a community or group to your site to buy; and the customer - the person buying costumes.

The goal is the have the publisher tell or show a network of people about your merchant website in an attempt to convert them into one of your customers. For any sales that result from this introduction on the publisher website about your business, the publisher will get a percentage of the sale. This is an example of a performance based sale. The more users of a publisher's website that they can convince to go to your website and make a purchase, the more you both make. The commission on the sale is always predetermined and each sale is tracked by the customers clicking on links that originate from the publisher's marketing campaign.

PAY PER CLICK

A publisher can also get paid on the number of clicks that lead from their website to your online costume shop through the same process and get paid by per visitor rather than on each sale. This process is called pay-per-click (PPC) and each visitor leads to payment. Google has a very established affiliate marketing program.

As a merchant you can use Google's affiliate marketing program Google Ad Word Space also known as pay-per-click (PPC). Paying Google per click on the key words allows you appear in the advertisement space at the top and the column to the right of the organic search. This slightly orange-pink box is paid advertising by companies. Once you choose the phrase you believe people will search for, then Google charges you based on how many other companies want to also appear for the same phrases. Google gets paid when someone clicks on the ad space. Clicks range from a few cents to over a dollar each, depending on how popular and how much you will pay for those key words. Be thrifty on the amount you spend on Google Ad Words, it can get expensive and you are not a guaranteed sale. Pay Per Click is a lead generator and a way of attracting customers, however it does not prevent a customer from opening multiple windows to window shop. Sixty five percent of people click on the ad space, but that leaves thirty five percent of people clicking on the organic search area. I recommend using Google Ad Words because Google has become the most popular search engines, hands down. Purchasing Google Ad Words is another way of showing up high in the Google search results.

SOCIAL MEDIA

Social Media amplifies everything you do onto a much larger audience, as informal short pieces of news and events for individuals and companies. Think of Social Media as old fashioned word of mouth, but with so many more ears listening. Social Media is built on short easy to read or view messages, in text or in video, frequently sent. Meaningful or fun messages will inform or share information, and let potential customers know that your only aim is not simply to sell costumes and accessories.

Social Media has captured the short attention span of Internet users to enable more people to talk to each other and connect. It is the most important free marketing tool available to you and you should be using it to promote your business. If you are not on any social network, now is the time to make your debut. If you are not sure you are ready for this kind of exposure, I'm not sure you are ready to succeed. Over 800 million people and companies are on Facebook. The largest growing users today are baby boomers.

Social Media will benefit your business in many ways as it:

a) **expands the reach of your company's products and services so you are able to find new customers.**
b) **allows you to identify and relate to your suppliers and influential people in the Halloween industry.**
c) **are able to keep tabs on your competitors.**

d) **gives you a platform to instantly connect with your customers and build a mutually interactive relationship.**

e) **gives you a low cost or free way to publish your message quickly and easily.**

f) **improves your Search Engine Optimization (SEO) because you have information flowing out.**

g) **publicizes events, deals and new products you offer.**

h) **functions as a substitute for a website if you need a quick start to creating a platform to place your information**

i) **helps you create better service, products and content as you learn receive online feedback from customers.**

Before you get started creating Social Media pages, create clear goals and measurable outcomes for your use of Social Media.so you have a strategy to benefit your business. Here are some important questions to ask to understand your goals:

- What type of relationship do you want to create with you customer?
- How will Social Media presence convert to sales on your own website?
- What images, videos and content do you plan to use or create to build your brand awareness?

- What do you want to learn about your competitors and customers by using Social Media?
- How will you manage the time needed to create and maintain a regular Social Media connection?

Once you have answers to these questions, they will guide your decisions, your voice and your interactions on all Social Media.

Social Media is constantly evolving because it is tied to technology. Competition among Social Media sites is fierce and creating a user experience that will keep users creating content and connecting with more people and businesses is the only way to survive.

TIP BOX: The many Social Media websites have meant many businesses and people spend too much time or get overloaded with maintaining their content and customers. Once you have an established social media presence, make time to update your site, but only once or twice a day for no more than 20 minutes before returning to other business matters. Or hire a Virtual Assistant (VA) to help schedule and find relevant content to post. Go to http://www.thehalloweenbusiness.com/book/va to learn about how I use my VA to help me save time and money.

To start a Halloween Social Media site, I recommend using Facebook, YouTube and Twitter. If you are more Social Media savvy or ambitious, add Pintrest, Google+ and Vimeo. All of your Social Media accounts for your business should be separate from your personal accounts.

Managing each of these sites is easier if you have the same message, video, and/or image sent to all your social networks. There are many programs that will post your content to each of your social networks at a push of a button. This will create a consistent message for each network and make it easier for you to manage. Here are timeless topics that you can recycle year after year just before Halloween:

- Popular costumes based on movies that came out that year
- How to recycle your old costume and still make it fresh for this year
- What to buy when you are on a budget
- How to go the extra mile with your make up and make you costume a hit
- The sexiest costumes of the season
- The cutest costumes for kids this year
-

The posts that you will create and use for each type of Social Media, should be no more than 140 character with images. This is the ideal length so people will read your content. Your posts should be written in a conversational tone. Initially you should try to create your own content and messages. But one of your goals should be to have users contribute to your content, tag photos and share videos on your Social Media websites. This frees you from having to create all the content.

TIP BOX: If you are still struggling to create your Social Media page, go to http://www.TheHalloweenBusiness.com/socialmedia to see an overview of my tips on creating both Halloween specific and year round messages and videos through social media.

FACEBOOK

Facebook is the largest source for a business to connect with potential customers. This is always the first place you need to post photos of your store and products. You should also allow customers to post photos of themselves and friends dressed in their favorite costumes that they have purchased from your business. Set up a Facebook Fan page for your Halloween Business and ask all of your friends to "Like" your Facebook Fan page. Post two or three pictures and status updates to start your page. When customers buy from you, ask them to like you on Facebook and to share fun tips on dressing up. Offer a discount on another purchase or an entry into a weekly costume contest if they tag your company in costumes they wear.

For brick and mortar stores, a great way to get more photos and traffic is to have a photo booth with a few costumes as props. Program the photo booth to have your store name and website in the lower corner and automatically let the person upload it to Facebook and any other social networks. This will allow you to have free publicity.

It is recommended that you post all new content and images (but not videos) it on Facebook first. Then use the reposting programs to post the same content, message or image to Twitter, Pinterest and Google+. Facebook wants to be the first place for original content. Facebook aims to be set apart from all other Social Media. So give the biggest social media network what they want, by posting your content first.

YOUTUBE

YouTube is the largest online video site and like Facebook wants to be the first place you upload new videos. So upload your video first to YouTube directly. Use the online reposting programs to post your video to other video sites. YouTube is incredibly powerful as we becoming more visually stimulated. Most people today would rather see a video than read a blog post. The first video you create should be a video about your company that tells your core story. You can be in front of the camera or use a puppet or professional actor in costume to introduce your company to the world, as long as your video is fun and creative. It will be a great way to start out your business online.

As you progress in your business, create a new video with a new creative twist at least once every year, to advertise for your business. This will allow you to stay in the eye of your customers. Keep your videos simple and short-one to two minutes per video and have a video editor add your logo and website into the introduction and end. Use your smart phone camera to make a quick video or hire a more professional crew if you have a budget. Informal videos are all over YouTube, so there is no shame in low budget advertising.

TWITTER

Twitter invented the 140 character long posts and tiny URLs so people could read more. There is so much information at our fingertips with the Internet that we have an attention span of a gnat. Social Media users only want the short version of everything they read but still get the full message. Writing 140 characters is enough to communicate a full idea if you are concise with your words. If they like your post, they will follow you on Twitter and may want to find out more about your company. If your 140 character post is for a blog entry on your website, they can use the Tiny URL link to read the rest of your article. Use Twitter to also follow other competitors in your industry and repost. This practice is referred to as *retweeting* content you like. Twitter is a great way to monitor how much work your competitors are doing and how many followers they have.

PINTEREST

This is a new popular image social network site that is devoted to posting, sharing, finding and pinning to your own space. It is one of the highest traffic areas for Halloween costumes, party ideas and pop culture images. Use this site to upload original images to your own space and re-pin images you like from others. When you pin a photo to your space, you are notified when other people re-pin your image to their space. This will indicate the popularity of an image as it gets passed around to other people's spaces. Pinterest uses the word pin to indicate that something has been placed on their board, or the space used to put the images. Pinterest has a lot of fashion, decorations, recipes and colorful photos from millions of users. Pinterest can be a virtual voting booth when you have costume images through the re-pinning of those images. When you get a lot of re-pinning of images, you will know what people like. This helps you find other images and other people to re-pin their images to your own space.

VIMEO

This is another great place to post videos you create. Although not at large as YouTube, Vimeo has millions of users and should not be overlooked. Vimeo has a reputation for attracting more creative and artsy users, who avoid uploading to YouTube. If you already have the content you may as well put it there. It is easy to upload videos to Vimeo.

GOOGLE+

Google+ is a new social network space that allows you create circles of friends and customers. You can organize your audience and speak directly to each group of people in your content and posts. Google+ allows you to manage the content and interactions intimately through those smaller group posts. You can upload video, images and written content to Google+.

The use of Social Media is a free marketing tool. The more you build the more people will come to you. But, it is time consuming to build social media networks. At first you may feel you are writing content, collecting images and creating videos for no audience except your friends. However that content is online permanently. Users will find you through the competitors you follow and by finding friends and people you want to follow. Stay active in the Social Media world and it will pay off in the long run. Get good at Social Media and if you are too busy to monitor this aspect of your business, hire a social media consultant to create content and find followers. If you are truly only working two months a year, you have ten months to build, follow and create a meaningful and active social media presence online. If you get too busy in September and October, then create content at an earlier date to be released during those months.

PART 3
CONCLUSION

AFTERWARD

I have given you the keys to success. It's time to take action. Starting a business is one of the most rewarding challenges in life. I have outlined a proven success path. The Halloween Business will create the work-life balance you have always wanted and build the financial freedom you deserve.

TIP BOX: Ready! What's Next? Go to my completion video to congradulate you on learning and implementing what you have read. www.thehalloweenbusiness.com/book/next

I meet many aspiring entrepreneurs who want to "try" business or have a great idea they have never pursued. They are looking for reassurance their idea is great, for guidance and for confidence. Your guide is here. The confidence to succeed is within you. Nobody else can give you confirmation and assure you of success, except you. People around you will either support you positively or negatively to your business endeavor, but you get the final word. Take action on your ideal life.

I wrote this book to cease the same great opportunity the Halloween Business represents in my life and gift it to you. I'm offering a life working 2 months per year and the ability to keep your job. It is what I have always wanted to do with my life. Cease this opportunity.

For more personalized programs, to start your business, I have entrepreneurial consulting programs to individualize your success. These programs build on this material and guide you to take regular action. These programs are available at TheHalloweenBusiness.com. A free strategy session will laser focus you and assess if you need additional consulting.

This is for you. Cease it.

WEBSITE RESOURCES

FROM THE HALLOWEEN BUSINESS BOOK

Welcome Video:

http://www.thehalloweenbusiness.com/book/welcome

Hire a Virtual Assistant:

http://www.thehalloweenbusiness.com/book/va

Catalog Costumes For Your Website:

http://www.thehalloweenbusiness.com/book/categorysearch

Halloween Costume Trends:

http://thehalloweenbusiness.com/book/trends

Hiring Freelance Help From The Internet:

www.thehalloweenbusiness.com/book/freelance

Using Social Media for Halloween

www.thehalloweenbusiness.com/socialmedia

I'm Ready! What's Next?

www.thehalloweenbusiness.com/book/next

ABOUT THE AUTHOR

SHANNON SHUE, entrepreneur and wanderlust, has been featured on NBC, CBS, FOX and other media. She has traveled the world and sought to learn and experience life usually read about in books. She has always had a love for dressing up in costume and business.

The Halloween Business is the culmination of over 5 years in sales and marketing for a large design and manufacturing company, where she started as the lowest sales person and worked her way up to the top sales person. It is through helping entrepreneurs from all over the world that teaches her how to create success for herself and others.

Shannon continues to build her TV personality and marketing strategies in Halloween through her websites www.TheHalloweenBusiness.com, where she helps entrepreneurs with video programs and consulting for success.

www.ingramcontent.com/pod-product-compliance
Lightning Source LLC
Chambersburg PA
CBHW060625210326
41520CB00010B/1478